W9-CAZ-124

Dr. Seuss's
'TIS THE

SEASON
A Holiday Celebration

Random House New York

'Tis the season!
It's time
to **Decorate** . . .

. . . and to
SEND GREETINGS
to family and friends.

'Tis the season
for **BAKING** . . .

. . . and for trying
OLD FAMILY RECIPES.

. . . and for families to COME TOGETHER.

'Tis the season to **HELP OTHERS** . . .

... and to raise
voices in **SONG**.

'Tis the season to **DREAM** about Santy Claus . . .

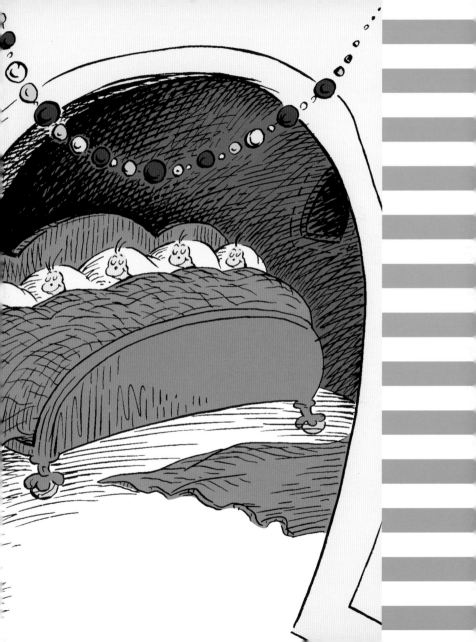

. . . and for children to **LAUGH** and **PLAY**.

'Tis the season
to **FEAST** . . .

. . . and to remember
the true meaning
of the holiday.
MERRY CHRISTMAS!

Maybe Christmas doesn't come from a store

Maybe Christmas doesn't come from a store